WETLAND BIRD SONGS & CALLS

Hannu Jännes
and Owen Roberts

WETLAND BIRD SONGS & CALLS

Hannu Jännes
and Owen Roberts

NEW
HOLLAND

First published in 2013 by New Holland Publishers
London • Cape Town • Sydney • Auckland
www.newhollandpublishers.com

Garfield House, 86–88 Edgware Road, London W2 2EA, UK
80 McKenzie Street, Cape Town 8001, South Africa
Unit 1, 66 Gibbes Street, Chatswood, New South Wales, Australia 2067
218 Lake Road, Northcote, Auckland, New Zealand

Copyright © 2013 in bird sounds: Hannu Jännes
Copyright © 2013 in text: Owen Roberts
Copyright © 2013 in photographs: AGAMI
Copyright © 2013 New Holland Publishers (UK) Ltd

3 5 7 9 10 8 6 4 2

A CIP catalogue record for this book is available from the British Library.

ISBN 978 1 78009 249 2

Publisher and editor: Simon Papps
Layout: Ann Pearlman

Production: Marion Storz
Printed and bound in China by Toppan Leefung Printing Ltd.

Other titles available in this series:
Bird Songs and Calls (ISBN 978 1 84773 779 3)
Common Garden Bird Calls (ISBN 978 1 84773 517 1)
Woodland Bird Songs and Calls (ISBN 978 1 78009 248 5)

CONTENTS

INSIDE BACK COVER
CD with bird sounds of 80 wetland species

INTRODUCTION TO WETLAND BIRD SOUNDS

My experience in more than 50 years of watching birds has convinced me that the easiest way to put a name to them is a familiarity with their songs and calls. After all, many of the species found in this book, although easy to identify when seen well, are often fully or at least partially hidden from view by grasses or reeds, or simply out of range on a distant waterline, to be visually identified with certainty. However, looking out over an apparently birdless marsh, you will almost certainly hear species such as Curlew and Redshank if they are present, and those distant white specks will doubtless be calling to reveal themselves as Black-headed Gulls. Indeed some species such as the crakes, and some of the warblers, found in this book are almost impossible to see, but by knowing their songs you can become aware of their presence.

Becoming familiar with the songs and calls of wetland birds does require some effort. Unlike songbirds, which defend territory and attract mates by song, many wetland birds establish territory by aggression towards rivals and find their partners by display. Very few are silent, though, especially during

the breeding season, and as they often have much larger territories than songbirds, it is easier to isolate sound emanating from a marsh than it is in a wood, where birds of several species can be singing in the same small patch.

The principle of early and late in the day applies to wetland species in just the same way as songbirds in woodland, possibly even more so as many birds such as crakes and rails are crepuscular in habits and most active at dawn and dusk. Visits at these times to your local wetland would be my recommendation, but choose days when there is little or no wind, when not only will birds be more likely to sing and call, but the sound will carry better too.

Do be aware that several of the birds described in these pages can sound very like amphibians or even insects – for example, a calling Baillon's Crake can sound very like an Edible Frog – so beware!

Now read the text and examine the wonderful photographs of birds to be found in these pages, but most of all listen to Hannu Jännes's fine recordings on the accompanying CD, as these will provide you with the easiest route along the road to being able to identify birds in the field.

OWEN ROBERTS

HOW TO USE THIS BOOK

• This book, together with the CD, teaches you to recognize some of the amazing sounds our birds make. The book features photographs and some information on each of the 80 birds. It tells you where to find them, if they are here all year or only visiting us, what they eat and how they nest.

• Use the CD with the book to match the pictures of the birds with the sounds they make. The track numbers on the CD correspond with the numbering of the birds in the book.

• As you learn and remember the sounds, you will be able to look for those birds when you hear them. Simply follow the call and look for the bird that is making it.

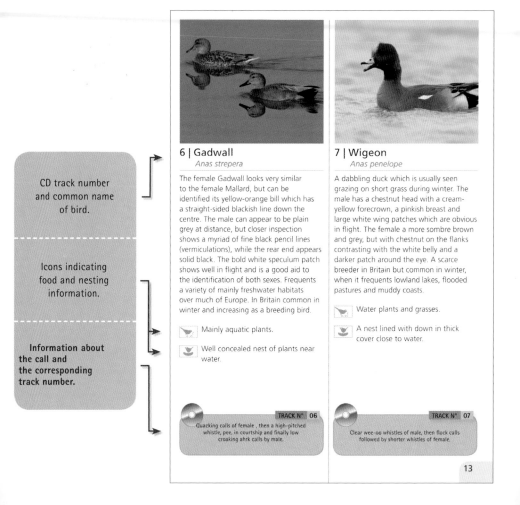

CD track number and common name of bird.

Icons indicating food and nesting information.

Information about the call and the corresponding track number.

6 | Gadwall
Anas strepera

The female Gadwall looks very similar to the female Mallard, but can be identified its yellow-orange bill which has a straight-sided blackish line down the centre. The male can appear to be plain grey at distance, but closer inspection shows a myriad of fine black pencil lines (vermiculations), while the rear end appears solid black. The bold white speculum patch shows well in flight and is a good aid to the identification of both sexes. Frequents a variety of mainly freshwater habitats over much of Europe. In Britain common in winter and increasing as a breeding bird.

Mainly aquatic plants.

Well concealed nest of plants near water.

TRACK N° 06
Quacking calls of female , then a high-pitched whistle, pee, in courtship and finally low croaking ahrk calls by male.

7 | Wigeon
Anas penelope

A dabbling duck which is usually seen grazing on short grass during winter. The male has a chestnut head with a cream-yellow forecrown, a pinkish breast and large white wing patches which are obvious in flight. The female a more sombre brown and grey, but with chestnut on the flanks contrasting with the white belly and a darker patch around the eye. A scarce breeder in Britain but common in winter, when it frequents lowland lakes, flooded pastures and muddy coasts.

Water plants and grasses.

A nest lined with down in thick cover close to water.

TRACK N° 07
Clear wee-oo whistles of male, then flock calls followed by shorter whistles of female.

13

1 | Greylag Goose
Anser anser

The plumage is brown-grey overall with a white undertail and flesh-coloured legs. In most of Europe the bill is plain orange, but the birds of some populations that breed in Russia have pinkish bills. In flight, Greylags can be easily identified by their strikingly pale forewings, which contrast strongly with a dark rear to the wing. Substantial feral populations are resident in many parts of Europe, including Britain, but truly wild birds migrate south and west in autumn. They breed mainly around shallow and freshwater marshes, but in winter are found on stubbles, pastures and saltmarshes.

 Plants in summer. Grass, grain and roots in winter.

 Large and unlined in rushes or other vegetation.

2 | Canada Goose
Branta canadensis

This large North American goose has become a firmly established feral breeder in Britain and other parts of Europe. The population originated from escaped collection birds, but occasional true vagrants do occur in Britain, particularly in south-west Scotland. It has a brown body with a very long black neck and tail and white cheek-patches that merge underneath the throat. The species occurs in all types of wetlands, including urban parks and lakes, and is one of the most vocal of all wildfowl, with its frequent loud honking calls.

 Grass, grain, clover and aquatic plants.

 Large structure of reeds, lined with down, usually on island in lake.

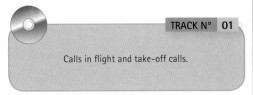

TRACK N° 01

Calls in flight and take-off calls.

TRACK N° 02

Excited, deep honking calls and warning calls.

3 | Mute Swan
Cygnus olor

This bird is familiar to all, often from childhood visits to parks and lakes. The Mute Swan is a very large white bird with a long neck and orange-red bill, which has a black knob at the base. At 152cm in length, it is the largest flying bird in Britain. Juveniles are grey-brown, becoming progressively more white as they mature, a process that takes about two years to complete.

When swimming, the Mute Swan looks very graceful, especially when the wings are partially raised either in threat or display, making it look like a stately white galleon as it glides effortlessly on the calm waters of a pond, lake or river. In flight, its wings make a loud throbbing sound. It is common across much of Europe, including Britain, where it is a common and widespread resident.

Although the Mute Swan can be very tame and takes bread from humans, it can be aggressive near the nest or when protecting its young, raising its wings and making grunting and hissing noises.

 Pulls up aquatic plants from shallow water. Usually feeds by dipping its neck below the surface of the water, sometimes by upending. Also grazes grasses on land.

A huge mound of aquatic vegetation close to water.

TRACK N° 03

Nasal *heeorr* calls, then the loud throbbing sound of wingbeats when in flight.

4 | Bewick's Swan
Cygnus bewickii

Our smallest swan, being only 10–15cm longer than a large Canada Goose, looks like a smaller version of the Whooper Swan. However, it can be identified by its much shorter neck, less elongated head shape and by the bill, which is mainly black with a restricted patch of yellow only at the base – with the Whooper, the yellow extends beyond the nostrils and close to the tip of the bill. The juvenile has grey-brown plumage and a pinkish bill.

It breeds only in north Russia and Siberia. It migrates south and west to spend the winter around the North Sea, Black Sea and Mediterranean. In Britain, it has a generally more southerly winter range than the Whooper, predominantly in England, and is largely absent from Scotland. It usually winters in family parties, which often join together to form flocks.

 Aquatic plants and grass. In winter also frequents farm fields to feast on spilt grain and root vegetables.

 A mound of vegetation by pools on Arctic tundra.

TRACK N° 05

Triumph and greeting calls, then flock calls in flight.

5 | Whooper Swan
Cygnus cygnus

The Whooper Swan is similar in length and wingspan to the Mute Swan, but less heavily built. The plumage of the adult is all white, though the head neck is often stained brown by the water they feed in. The best clues to identity are that the neck is frequently held straight, not curved as is often the case with the Mute Swan, and the bill is largely bright yellow rather than orange. The majority of the bill is yellow, with a black tip, whereas the Bewick's Swan has a much more extensive area of black extending up beyond the nostrils.

The Whooper breeds on lakes and tundra pools in the far north of Europe, including Scandinavia, Russia and Iceland, and there are a few pairs in Scotland. It migrates south for the winter, with good numbers in Britain, especially Scotland. It is a very vocal species, with loud trumpeting and bugling. Its wings do not make a throbbing noise in flight as they do with the Mute Swan.

 Aquatic plants and grass. Also takes grain and root vegetables from agricultural fields in winter.

A large mound of vegetation by the waterside.

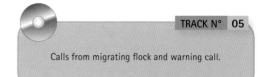

TRACK N° 05

Calls from migrating flock and warning call.

6 | Gadwall
Anas strepera

The female Gadwall looks very similar to the female Mallard, but can be identified by its yellow-orange bill, which has a straight-sided blackish line down the centre. The male can appear to be plain grey at a distance, but closer inspection shows a myriad of fine, black pencil lines (vermiculations), while the rear end appears solid black. The bold white speculum patch shows well in flight and is a good aid to the identification of both sexes. It frequents a variety of mainly freshwater habitats over much of Europe. In Britain, it is common in winter and increasing as a breeding bird.

 Mainly aquatic plants.

 Well concealed nest of plants near water.

7 | Wigeon
Anas penelope

A dabbling duck, the Wigeon is usually seen grazing on short grass during winter. The male has a chestnut head with a cream-yellow forecrown, a pinkish breast and large, white wing patches that are obvious in flight. The female is a more sombre brown and grey, but with chestnut on the flanks, contrasting with the white belly and a darker patch around the eye. It is a scarce breeder in Britain but common in winter, when it frequents lowland lakes, flooded pastures and muddy coasts.

 Water plants and grasses.

 A nest lined with down in thick cover close to water.

TRACK N° 06

Quacking calls of female, then a high-pitched whistle, *pee*, in courtship and finally low croaking *ahrk* calls by male.

TRACK N° 07

Clear *wee-oo* whistles of male, then flock calls followed by shorter whistles of female.

8 | Mallard
Anas platyrhynchos

By far Europe's commonest duck, it breeds wherever there is a freshwater habitat. The male sports a bottle-green head with a white collar, chestnut breast and greyish body. By contrast, the female is mottled brown and buff overall. Both sexes share a white-bordered purple-blue speculum (a patch in the wing) that shows well in flight.

 Upends in the water to take aquatic plants and invertebrates, but will often take bread from humans.

 Nest of grass and dead leaves in thick cover close to water.

9 | Shoveler
Anas clypeata

This species is characterized by a massive spatulate bill. The male has a glossy dark-green head, a white breast, chestnut flanks, and a black back and stern. The female is a mix of mottled browns. Shovelers are not uncommon on shallow lakes, marshland meadows and flooded grasslands. Numbers in Britain are swelled in winter by immigrants from north-east Europe and Iceland.

 Seeds and aquatic plants, small crustaceans, molluscs and insects. Feeds in shallow water, sieving food through its bill.

Nest is well concealed in often dry vegetation, but with water close by.

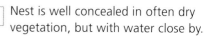
TRACK N° 08
Series of loud quacks by female followed by lower-pitched calls of male and finally quieter calls of a displaying flock including sharp *wiu* whistle by male when guarding female.

TRACK N° 09
Nasal, disyllabic call of male, then call of female, followed by calls of agitated birds.

10 | Pintail
Anas acuta

This elegant dabbling duck breeds by moorland pools and lakes in northern Europe, but it is a scarce breeder in Britain. It is much more common here in winter, when it frequents estuaries and flooded fens, especially around the coasts. The male has a chocolate-brown head, white neck, mainly grey body and white belly. The female is rather like a pale female Mallard, but has an obvious grey bill. Both sexes appear rather slim and long-necked and have pointed tails, with long central feathers on the male.

 Aquatic plants and invertebrates.

In short cover by water.

11 | Common Teal
Anas crecca

Europe's smallest duck is resident in fresh and brackish water habitats in Britain. In winter the population swells due to migrants arriving from the north and east. The male's body appears mainly grey and the head is a rich chestnut with a yellow-framed, metallic green patch around the eye. The female is streaked and mottled brown and buff. Both sexes have a bright green speculum that is conspicuous in flight.

 Mainly aquatic invertebrates in the breeding season and seeds and plants in winter.

 Nest of grass and sedges is lined with down and situated in thick cover.

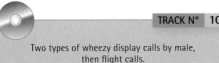

TRACK N° 10

Two types of wheezy display calls by male, then flight calls.

TRACK N° 11

Peeping calls of male, calls from flock including clear peep calls by males and quack calls of females. Finally, warning calls by female.

12 | Pochard
Aythya ferina

The Pochard is a medium-sized diving duck that is scarce as a breeder in Britain but common in winter, when the population increases with migrants from northern and eastern Europe. The handsome drake has a grey back, a black chest and stern, and a bright chestnut head with a black bill that has a grey band. Females have a similar pattern, but of dull greys and browns. Pochards are usually seen on larger lakes and reservoirs. They feed mainly by dabbling and diving.

 Aquatic plants and insects, molluscs and small fish.

Bulky, of rank vegetation close to water.

13 | Tufted Duck
Aythya fuligula

The most common diving duck in Britain, this dapper black-and-white drake has a head tuft that is longer in spring than at other times. The female is similarly patterned, but brown replaces the black and grey-brown the white. The bill is blue with a black tip in adults of both sexes. Tufted Ducks are common inland on lakes and large ponds, especially in winter when they also frequent saltwater habitats.

 Dives for invertebrates and aquatic plants.

 Nest of dry grass and sedges is lined with down and hidden in thick cover near water.

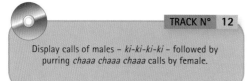

TRACK N° 12

Display calls of males – *ki-ki-ki-ki* – followed by purring *chaaa chaaa chaaa* calls by female.

TRACK N° 13

First the bubbling courtship call of the male, then a long rhythmic series of sharp notes, *ghik-ghik-ghik-ghik*, from the female.

14 | Goldeneye
Bucephala clangula

This diving duck spends most of its life on lakes, reservoirs, large rivers and sheltered coasts. The male is black and white, with the large white spot behind the bill being an obvious field mark. The female has a mostly grey body with a white collar round the neck and a brown head. The wings, which show a large white patch in flight, make a whistling sound as they beat. Fairly common and widespread in Britain in winter, it is slowly colonizing northern parts as a breeding bird.

 Dives for molluscs, crustaceans and insect larvae.

 Nests in a tree hole or nestbox close to water in forested areas of northern Europe.

15 | Goosander
Mergus merganser

This large duck belongs to the family known as sawbills, which is so named because their bills have serrated edges to enable them to grasp slippery fish. The male is a handsome bird, mainly white with a glossy greenish-black head, a red bill and black back. The female is mainly grey with a white chin and a brown head with a shaggy crest down the nape. It winters and breeds in similar habitats to Goldeneye, but has a more widely distributed breeding range in Britain.

 Feeds almost exclusively on fish.

 Nests in a hole in a tree close to water.

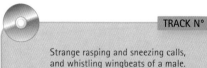

TRACK N° 14

Strange rasping and sneezing calls, and whistling wingbeats of a male.

TRACK N° 15

Display call of male, *koo-kot*, then *tra-ta-ta* of female, with male audible in background.

16 | Red-throated Diver
Gavia stellata

Divers are large, long-necked birds with paddle-shaped feet set well to the rear of their bodies, so whilst they are superb swimmers, they are ill-equipped for life on land, which they only visit to nest. The Red-throated is Europe's smallest diver, although it is still as large as a small goose. For much of the year the plumage is blackish-brown above with whitish spots and speckles, while the underparts, neck and face are all whitish. However, in the breeding season both sexes moult into a very distinctive plumage with a plain, dark-brown body and a grey head and neck, which is finely striped black and white to the rear, with a ruby throat patch at the front.

It breeds in northern Europe, including Scotland and Northern Ireland, on moorland lochs and tundra pools. It spends winter on the sea, often close inshore, and is widespread around all British coasts.

 Dives for fish, and occasionally takes other aquatic animals.

Nest is situated on the ground, often on an islet and never far from water's edge.

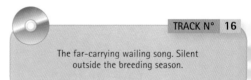

TRACK N° 16

The far-carrying wailing song. Silent outside the breeding season.

17 | Black-throated Diver
Gavia arctica

A little larger than the Red-throated Diver, but the bill of the Black-throated is usually held horizontally rather than slightly tilted upwards as in the Red-throated. In winter plumage, the Black-throated Diver is white below, but the upperparts are blackish-brown without any speckling. The white fore-neck is sharply demarcated from the blackish rear neck and crown. When swimming, there is a distinctive large white patch on the rear of the flanks.

During the summer months, the plumage on the body is a stunning mix of stripes and chequering in blacks, greys and whites. The head and hind-neck are plain grey and the black throat-patch is bordered by fine, vertical black-and-white striping.

It breeds on deeper, larger lakes than the Red-throated Diver, and its breeding range extends across northern Europe, including northern and western Scotland. It spends winter in coastal waters and is sometimes found inland on large lakes and reservoirs.

Dives for fish.

Nests in a shallow depression situated in herbage, often on an islet.

TRACK N° 17

Loud, evocative song and two types of call.
Silent outside breeding season.

18 | Little Grebe
Tachybaptus ruficollis

Britain's smallest grebe is both small and dumpy, with a powder-puff rear end. In winter it is a rather nondescript brown and buff, but in the breeding season the plumage is mainly blackish-brown with chestnut cheeks and fore-neck, and a bright yellow gape. It is widespread and common on well-vegetated lakes, ponds and rivers. In winter it is also found on more open waters, including reservoirs and sheltered coasts. Little Grebes are well known for their loud 'whinnying' call. Pairs display in duet.

 Fish, aquatic insects, small molluscs, tadpoles. Dives to catch prey.

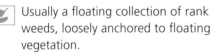 Usually a floating collection of rank weeds, loosely anchored to floating vegetation.

19 | Slavonian Grebe
Podiceps auritus

The Slavonian Grebe is intermediate in size between the Great Crested and Little Grebes. In summer it has a black head with golden plumes raised above the top of the crown (earning its American name of Horned Grebe), while the neck, breast and flanks are deep chestnut. In winter it looks blackish above, with paler flanks and neck, and a black crown with a sharply defined border against a white cheek. It breeds in northern Europe – including northern Scotland – on lakes and ponds with well-vegetated margins. It winters on sheltered coasts and estuaries around the UK, and also on large lakes and reservoirs.

 Dives for small fish, aquatic insects, molluscs.

 Of decomposing vegetation in aquatic herbage by water's edge.

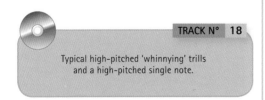

TRACK N° 18

Typical high-pitched 'whinnying' trills and a high-pitched single note.

TRACK N° 19

Advertising calls made by displaying birds.
Silent in winter.

20 | Great Crested Grebe
Podiceps cristatus

This large, elegant grebe is similar in length to a Mallard. It has a long, slender neck that is usually held erect, and a long pinkish bill. In winter, the plumage has a white face and fore-neck, black crown, pale brown flanks and dark-brown back and hind-neck. When breeding it develops a blackish double crest on the crown, while below the cheeks are brownish-red head plumes that have black tips. The young, like the young of all European grebe species, have the head boldly striped black and white like a humbug.

The species has a spectacular series of courtship displays that includes a dance on water, and pairs indulge in head-shaking and a 'weed dance'. It breeds on larger lakes surrounded by reeds, and winters on open lakes and reservoirs or sheltered coastal waters. Common throughout most of Britain, its breeding range extends across most of Europe, with northern breeders moving south in winter.

Small fish, frogs, molluscs and aquatic insects, which it catches by diving.

Builds a large floating structure of wet, decayed weeds and reeds, loosely moored to aquatic vegetation.

TRACK N° 20

Various loud bleating and clucking calls from a breeding colony.

21 | Red-necked Grebe
Podiceps grisegena

22 | Black-necked Grebe
Podiceps nigricollis

The Red-necked Grebe is slightly smaller than the Great Crested Grebe, and with a shorter, thicker neck. It is not dissimilar in winter plumage, but has a grey neck contrasting with a white throat and breast, and a dark bill with a yellow base, rather than an all-pink bill. In summer, the cheeks become grey and its neck and breast chestnut. It breeds on shallow, well-vegetated lakes and ponds, mainly in Eastern Europe and Finland, but moves south and west to winter on sheltered coasts and estuaries, including those in eastern Britain.

The Black-necked Grebe is similar in size to the Slavonian, but its shape is more like the Little Grebe. In summer it has a black neck and head, with wispy golden-yellow ear-plumes (hence on the cheeks rather than on top of the head, as with the Slavonian). In winter the fore-neck is greyer than that of the Slavonian and the black crown extends onto the cheek as a dark smudge. In summer it frequents shallow, well-vegetated ponds and lakes. It is a rare breeder in Britain, but more widespread in winter, when it often forms loose flocks on lakes, reservoirs and estuaries.

 Dives for small fish, aquatic insects, molluscs and crustaceans.

 Dives to catch fish and aquatic insects.

 Breeds colonially, building a rank floating heap in emergent vegetation at waterside.

Floating heap of aquatic weeds anchored to vegetation.

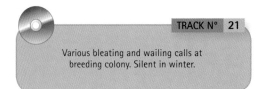

TRACK N° 21

Various bleating and wailing calls at breeding colony. Silent in winter.

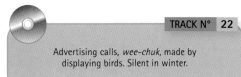

TRACK N° 22

Advertising calls, *wee-chuk*, made by displaying birds. Silent in winter.

23 | Cormorant
Phalacrocorax carbo

This large bird is often seen perched with its wings open, looking like a creature from prehistory. The breeding adult's plumage is glossy black overall, but with white patches on the throat and thigh, and bare yellow skin around the bill.

In breeding plumage, the inland race *sinensis* develops much white on the crown and neck – these birds are tree-nesters by lakes and large rivers and are found in scattered colonies throughout much of Europe, including southern Britain. In Britain, the nominate race, with a dark crown and neck, is a common breeding bird associated with the coast.

Outside the breeding season adults have all black plumage except for the white throat patch. Young birds of both races are dark brown and have a paler, sometimes even whitish, belly and breast.

Cormorants can be found in all sorts of wetlands, from large rivers, lakes and reservoirs to small streams and ponds. They often roost out of water, perched on the ground, on islands or in the branches of trees.

 Dives under water to catch fish.

 Breeds colonially in trees overhanging water. The nest a bulky, untidy structure of sticks and reeds.

TRACK N° 23

Typical calls of adults, then persistent calls of juveniles.

24 | Bittern
Botaurus stellaris

During spring the Bittern is more often heard than seen, thanks to its far-carrying 'booming' song. It is a large, thick-set heron which, due to its secretive nature, is often hard to see in its favoured habitat of extensive reed beds.

The cryptic plumage of rich buff, barred and streaked with black, makes ideal camouflage for the Bittern against a backdrop of reeds. On the ground, when disturbed, it often stands motionless, with neck outstretched and bill pointing skywards, blending perfectly with its surroundings.

The most frequent view of the bird is in low flight across a marsh, as it moves from one reed stand to another. The flight silhouette is very distinctive, with the appearance of a heron, but with a rather slow flight that is somewhat reminiscent to that of an owl.

Bitterns breed locally across Europe, except in the far north. In Britain, it is a scarce and localized breeding bird, although numbers have increased significantly in recent years so that there are now more than 100 'booming' males. Populations in Eastern Europe are migratory and these birds move south and west for the winter, supplementing the British population during this season.

 Stalks fish, frogs and other small animals.

 A large platform of reeds in extensive reed beds.

TRACK N° 24

Booming song followed by rather gull-like squawking flight calls.

25 | Grey Heron
Ardea cinerea

Europe's largest, commonest and most widespread heron, the Grey Heron is resident in Britain and can occur almost anywhere near water. It is grey above and whitish below, with a snake-like neck and a strong, dagger-shaped orange-yellow bill. Adults have black stripes to the sides of the crown. In flight, the wingbeats are slow and ponderous, and the bird looks huge with bowed wings and its long neck retracted. It usually nests colonially in trees. Adults display around the nest platforms, employing bill snapping and a variety of harsh calls. The young in nests maintain continuous loud, clicking calls.

 Fish, amphibians, insects and small mammals and birds.

 Colonially, building a large platform of sticks in a tree.

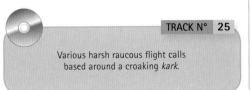

TRACK N° 25

Various harsh raucous flight calls based around a croaking *kark*.

26 | Little Egret
Egretta garzetta

Little Egrets have colonized southern Britain in the last 20 years, where the species is now a common resident in a variety of wetland habitats, including rivers, lakes, gravel pits, and coastal marshes and estuaries. The plumage is pure white, with a grey-black bill and legs, and yellow eyes and feet. In the breeding season it develops long, wispy, white plumes on the nape, breast and back. It nests colonially in trees, often with other heron species.

 Fish, frogs, large insects.

 Breeds colonially, building bulky stick nests in trees.

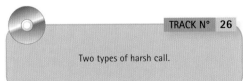

TRACK N° 26

Two types of harsh call.

25

27 | Osprey
Pandion haliaetus

The Osprey is a large fish-eating raptor famous for plunging spectacularly into the water to catch its prey. It spends the winter in Africa and migrates to northern parts of Europe to breed. Following extinction in Britain, it has now re-established itself well as a breeding species in Scotland and is gradually colonizing England and Wales. It breeds in places where there are conifers in which to nest and nearby lakes, rivers or ponds for food. The plumage is dark brown above, with white underparts. The head is white with a dark-brown stripe through the eye.

 Fish, which are caught by plunge-diving.

 Often exposed on the top of a large pine.

28 | White-tailed Eagle
Haliaeetus albicilla

This huge fish-eating eagle has an impressively large bill. Its plumage is mottled brown. Adults have a paler head, a pale yellow bill and a white wedge-shaped tail. However, these features only develop slowly and birds do not achieve full adult plumage for six or even seven years – immatures have a brownish tail, greyish bill and darker brown head. It looks enormous in flight, with rectangular wings uniformly broad throughout their length. It inhabits rocky coasts and larger lakes and rivers. Widely, but thinly, distributed over much of Northern Europe, it has been successfully reintroduced to western Scotland following extinction.

 Mainly fish, but will take birds as large as a goose in the air.

 A huge stick structure on a cliff or in a tree.

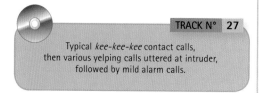

TRACK N° 27

Typical *kee-kee-kee* contact calls, then various yelping calls uttered at intruder, followed by mild alarm calls.

TRACK N° 28

Yelping calls near nest. Usually silent outside breeding season.

29 | Marsh Harrier
Circus aeruginosus

The Marsh Harrier is immediately recognizable as a harrier, thanks to its wavering, low, hunting flight with upraised wings and a long tail. The female is mostly dark brown with a creamy crown, throat and leading edges to the wing. The smaller male gradually acquires areas of pale grey on the wings and tail, while a mature male's underwings are almost entirely plain grey-buff, contrasting with the black wing-tips. The juvenile is similar to the female but darker brown in general with more yellow-buff markings on the crown and throat, and with no pale markings on the forewings.

It is primarily a summer visitor from Africa to much of Europe, but largely resident in the west of the range, including in Britain, western France and Iberia. Breeding is confined to reed beds, but it often hunts over more open country. The species is polygamous and one male may mate with several females. It almost became extinct as a British breeding bird due to hunting and pesticides, but in the past few decades it has recovered well and there are now several hundred nests each year.

 Small mammals, birds, eggs and nestlings of other waterbirds.

 On the ground in a reed bed or arable field.

TRACK N° 29

Calls of male during display flight, then excited soliciting perch calls of female followed by chattering calls of male.

27

30 | Water Rail
Rallus aquaticus

The Water Rail is a resident of reed beds and other dense aquatic vegetation in Western Europe, but those breeding in the east migrate west to winter and are capable of long migrations despite their weak-looking fluttery flight. Its pig-like squeal is often heard, but the bird is secretive by habit, generally only emerging from deep cover during hard winter weather. Dumpy in shape, it looks like a small Moorhen with a long red bill and long sturdy legs. It is brown with blackish streaking above and plain blue-grey on the face and breast. The flanks and belly are boldly barred black and white and the undertail is white. It is the only long-billed rail or crake found in Britain and the rest of Europe, although beware of shorter-billed juveniles, which could be mistaken for crakes.

Food in winter consists mainly of aquatic plant matter such as shoots, roots and seeds, and particularly in summer the diet is supplemented with invertebrates including insects, worms and crustaceans.

Nest is often constructed over water in densely vegetated locations such as reed- or sedge-beds. It is usually raised above the water on a platform of bent and broken reed stems.

TRACK N° 30

First the *kick-kick-kick* courtship song, which is used by both sexes, then the 'squealing pig' call of the male, which is used for display, alarm and territorial purposes.

31 | Baillon's Crake
Porzana pusilla

This tiny crake is a summer visitor to Europe. It is currently regarded as a vagrant to Britain, but several singing birds were found in 2012, suggesting that it may breed here. The sexes are similar and resemble the male Little Crake, but Baillon's has extensive barring on the flanks and an all-green bill with no red at the base. It is found in a wide variety of wet habitats that have a profusion of vegetation. It is an inveterate skulker and is best located by its song, which is given most frequently at night.

 Seeds of aquatic plants and small invertebrates.

A neat cup in a tussock usually surrounded by shallow water.

32 | Little Crake
Porzana parva

The Little Crake is Starling-sized, but with a crake's typical dumpy body shape. The male is basically brown above and blue-grey below with barring on the undertail. The female is similar, but with the blue-grey replaced by a buff belly and breast, white throat and pale lilac around the face. Both sexes have barred undertails, yellowish-green bills with red at the base, and greenish legs. It occurs in dense reed beds with quite deep water, as it swims more frequently than its close relatives. A summer visitor found mainly in Eastern Europe, it is a very rare visitor to Britain.

 Seeds of aquatic plants and small invertebrates.

 A shallow cup in thick vegetation in, or close to, water.

 TRACK N° **31**

Song is a quiet, creaking, rasping *krrrre* repeated every two seconds in a long series (beware confusion with the similar-sounding Edible Frog).

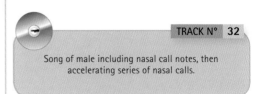 TRACK N° **32**

Song of male including nasal call notes, then accelerating series of nasal calls.

33 | Spotted Crake
Porzana porzana

The Spotted Crake is smaller than the Water Rail and with similar secretive habits to that species and to the other smaller two species of crakes. It breeds thoughout most of Europe but is rather a rare and localized breeder in Britain. It is a summer visitor that winters mostly in tropical Africa. It occurs more widely in Britain during migration but is still scarce.

The plumage is predominantly brown with darker streaking. There is some blue-grey on the face, breast and belly with, as the name suggests, a covering of fine white spotting all over the head and body. The undertail is plain buff, the thick legs are greenish and the bill is yellow with a red base.

The Spotted Crake occurs less frequently in reed beds than the Water Rail, preferring marshes and watercourses with low water levels and a dense covering of rushes and sedges. The loud 'whiplash' song is often the best clue to its presence at a site.

 Plants and invertebrates.

 In dense vegetation or in a tussock over shallow water.

TRACK N° 33

Two examples of the characteristic 'whiplash' song, which can carry as far as a mile on calm evenings.

34 | Moorhen
Gallinula chloropus

This common and often conspicuous bird has a variety of habitats, including ponds, small lakes, waterside meadows, canals, and slow-moving rivers and streams that have nearby dense vegetation. It is resident in Britain and other parts of southern and Western Europe, while more easterly breeders are short-distance migrants that winter in milder climes.

The plumage of the adult is mainly blackish-brown above and slate-grey on the head underparts, with conspicuous white patches under the tail and a broken white line along the flanks. The bill is bright red with a yellow tip and the legs are bright greenish-yellow. Juveniles –

which are like brown versions of the adults, with a paler face and a greyish bill – will sometimes help to raise the chicks of subsequent broods.

Moorhens swim with a series of jerky head and tail movements, and when feeding on land they walk and peck in a hen-like way.

 Aquatic plants, molluscs, insects, worms, seeds and grass.

 Nest is a well-woven platform built of reeds, grass and sedges situated in dense vegetation just out of water.

TRACK N° 34

The nasal *prrruwkk* advertising call of the male, crowing calls, a single, soft alarm call and confrontation calls including a sharp, rubber toy-like *kwe-ick*.

35 | Coot
Fulica atra

Larger than the Moorhen, the Coot is a familiar black waterbird that has a conspicuous white bill with a white frontal shield above it. It breeds in most open freshwater habitats that have surrounding vegetation in which to nest and shelter, including lakes, slow-moving rivers and canals with well-vegetated surrounds. However, outside the breeding season it often forms very large flocks on more open lakes, reservoirs and estuaries.

When swimming, the Coot employs a noticeable forwards nod of the head with each paddle, and it frequently dives to search for food. On land its pale-grey legs and huge, lobed toes are conspicuous.

The Coot is a common resident in Western Europe, including Britain, where numbers increase dramatically in winter with migration from further north and east.

Dives for water plants, aquatic invertebrates and small animal matter.

Constructs a large structure of reeds and sedges in waterside vegetation, sometimes actually in the water, but raised above it.

TRACK N° 35

Various calls given in spring, including an explosive *piip*, a short sharp *kuh* and a quite loud and often repeated *egh-ekh-ekh-ekh*.

36 | Common Crane
Grus grus

This very large bird has long legs and neck, and a graceful walk. It is famed for its evocative bugling call and for its spectacular spring dancing display. In recent years the species has begun a slow recolonization of Britain, with a small resident population centred in the Norfolk Broads, and the birds are also regularly seen at Lakenheath Fen RSPB reserve just across the border in Suffolk.

The bulk of the European population breeds in the marshes and bogs of northern and north-eastern Europe, spending the winter in Iberia and North Africa. They often migrate in large flocks in V-formation or diagonal lines; cranes look huge when flying with neck outstretched, which is a good way of distinguishing them from the Grey Heron, which always folds its neck back in flight.

The plumage is grey overall, while the head and neck of the adult are mostly black, with a bold white stripe from the red eye down the nape and a warty, red patch on the crown. The juvenile differs from the adult in having a greyish-brown head that blends in to the plumage of the body.

 Plants, spilt grain, insects and small mammals.

A huge mound of rank vegetation.

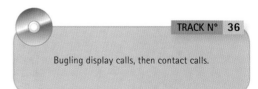

37 | Lapwing
Vanellus vanellus

Large flocks of Lapwings are a common sight in winter on open fields and marshes, but the birds' spectacular springtime aerobatic displays over rough pastures are now much less commonly seen than they once were due to changes in farming methods. The common country name of 'Peewit' is onomatopoeic and is derived from an interpretation of its call.

The bird is distinctive, with unique iridescent-green upperparts that look blackish from a distance, a black breast-band, face-patch and crown, topped by a long and whispy erectile crest. The sides of the head, lower breast and belly are white, the undertail is orange and the legs are pink. In flight, the broad wings and 'flappy' flight make the Lapwing relatively easy to identify; in spring it is frequently seen tumbling over open land in ecstatic display flight.

 Mainly adult and larval insects, spiders, snails and worms, occasionally plant matter such as seeds.

 Nest is a simple, sparsely lined scrape in grass or on bare ground in pasture or on arable land.

TRACK N° 37

Song and wingbeats from male in display flight, then warning calls by adult bird.

38 | Golden Plover
Pluvialis apricaria

In winter, the Golden Plover is found in large flocks on wet fields and estuaries, but in summer, when it sports golden-spangled upperparts and a black face, breast and belly, it breeds on moors, upland pastures and mountains. It has a plaintive whistling call evocative of wild places. In Britain, numbers increase considerably in winter with migrants from colder regions.

 Mainly insects and worms, with some seeds and berries. Feeds extensively at night.

Nest is a simple scrape in heather or rough grass.

39 | Little Ringed Plover
Charadrius dubius

This wading bird is a summer visitor from Africa. It first bred in Britain – where it is confined to sand and gravel areas by fresh water – as recently as 1938, doubtless aided by the proliferation of gravel pits in modern times. It is very similar to the more common Ringed Plover, but smaller with dull pinkish-grey legs, a yellow orbital eye-ring and an all-dark bill. In flight it is easily distinguished from the Ringed Plover because it lacks this species' wing-bar.

 Mainly invertebrates.

Nest is a simple scrape in sand or gravel. Characteristically of plovers, parents may feign a broken wing to divert predators if they sense a threat to their young.

TRACK N° 38

Rhythmical wailing *per-ooo per-ooo* song given by male in display flight, trilling *whe-wheedli'whe-wheedli...* song and alarm calls.

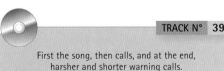

TRACK N° 39

First the song, then calls, and at the end, harsher and shorter warning calls.

40 | Avocet
Recurvirostra avosetta

One of the biggest conservation success stories in Britain during the 20th century, the Avocet was extinct as a breeding bird in this country until it returned to the Suffolk coast in the 1940s and was encouraged by the RSPB; the species is now the emblem for the society.

Today it is seen throughout the year in Britain at a number of favoured breeding and wintering localities. It breeds in marshy shore meadows and around seashores close to shallow water, where it feeds by wading and sweeping its bill from side to side to detect food by touch. It winters in flocks on muddy estuaries.

Elsewhere in Europe, more northerly breeders from Denmark and the Low Countries migrate south to winter in Iberia and as far south as West Africa. Thousands congregate in late summer to moult in the Waddenzee area.

In terms of identification, it is a fairly large, quite unmistakable, black-and-white wading bird with a slender, upcurved black bill and long, pale-bluish legs.

 Aquatic insects and crustaceans.

A lined scrape on bare ground near water.

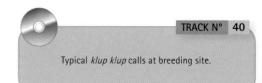

TRACK N° 40

Typical *klup klup* calls at breeding site.

41 | Common Sandpiper
Actitis hypoleucos

Brown above and white below, with densely streaked sides to its breast, when seen the Common Sandpiper crouches forwards and constantly bobs its rather elongated rear. Its flight involves rapid wingbeats interspersed with short glides, showing white wing-bars and calling constantly. A summer visitor from Africa, it breeds along upland streams, riverbanks and lake shores, but on passage it can be seen in all wetland habitats, including coasts and estuaries.

 Small molluscs, crustaceans, insects and worms.

Nest is a scrape in sand or gravel close to water.

42 | Green Sandpiper
Tringa ochropus

The Green Sandpiper is common on passage and in winter around freshwater habitats in much of Western Europe, including Britain, and also around the Mediterranean. As a breeding bird, its range is confined to the waterlogged forests of northern Europe, where it nests in trees. It has a mostly dark blackish-brown head, breast and upperparts with variable fine white spotting. It is often seen flying away when flushed, calling as it rises, and looking rather like a large House Martin with a blackish back contrasting with a prominent white rump. When seen on the ground, it habitually bobs its rear-end.

 Insects, molluscs, crustaceans, worms.

 Deserted squirrel dreys or old thrush nests in trees.

TRACK N° 41

First the trilling song, then a single *tsee-wee-wee* flight call, followed by a series of alarm calls.

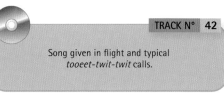

TRACK N° 42

Song given in flight and typical *tooeet-twit-twit* calls.

43 | Wood Sandpiper
Tringa glareola

A little bigger than the Common Sandpiper, it has much longer, yellow-green, legs. The upperparts are brown with paler spotting, the belly white, the breast and head diffusely streaked with brown, and there is a well-marked supercilium. In flight it shows a prominent white rump and pale underwings. A summer visitor that winters in Africa, it nests commonly on the bogs and marshes of northern Europe, but in Britain only rarely in northern Scotland. On migration, when it is widespread but still fairly scarce in Britain, it frequents marshes and flooded meadows.

 Insects, worms, molluscs.

 A scrape in dense ground vegetation.

44 | Marsh Sandpiper
Tringa stagnatilis

The Marsh Sandpiper is very like a Greenshank in plumage, but much smaller in every respect, especially the bill, which is fine and straight. In flight, it also resembles a miniature Greenshank, but the toes project very noticeably beyond the tail. It winters in Africa and Asia and formerly bred only in the far east of Europe, but in recent times it has extended its range west and now breeds sparsely in Poland and the Baltic States on grassy floods and marshes. It migrates in a south-easterly direction, so rare in Western Europe, and is a vagrant to Britain.

 Small invertebrates.

A shallow depression in short vegetation.

TRACK N° 43

Song, warning calls and contact calls.

TRACK N° 44

A series of typical calls, rather like a faster, higher-pitched version of the Greenshank's.

38

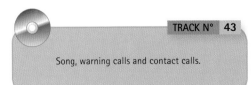

45 | Redshank
Tringa totanus

The Redshank is one of the most common and familiar waders in Britain. Mainly coastal in winter and on migration, it breeds inland on wet meadows and grass moors as well as on coastal marshes. It commonly breeds in northern and Eastern Europe, with birds from many of these populations wintering to the south and west. It is found throughout the year in Britain, although the population is supplemented by migrants during winter.

A medium-sized wader, the Redshank is grey-brown above and white below, becoming darker and heavily streaked with dark brown when breeding. As the name suggests, it has orange-red legs and it also has a red base to the bill. In flight, it is easily identified thanks to a white wedge-shape on its back and the broad white triangles on the trailing edges to the wings. Juveniles are paler and have yellow-orange legs, which can frequently lead to confusing it with other species such as the Wood Sandpiper.

 Mainly molluscs and crustaceans, but insects when breeding.

 Nest is a dome of woven grasses located in a dry place close to water.

TRACK N° 45

First a monosyllabic *tjuu* and disyllabic *tjuu-u* calls, then the song.

46 | Spotted Redshank
Tringa erythropus

The Spotted Redshank breeds on bogs in the very far north of Arctic Europe and winters coastally on shallow marshes, estuaries and saltpans, mainly around the Mediterranean, but also sheltered coasts in Western Europe, including Britain. This medium-sized, very elegant wader has long red legs and a long neck and bill. The bill is red at the base and black at the tip. In winter the plumage is very pale grey above and white below, but in spring the whole body becomes black, with very fine, white speckling on the upperparts.

 Molluscs, crustaceans, worms and insects.

 Nest is a shallow depression on the ground in short vegetation.

47 | Greenshank
Tringa nebularia

This fairly large wading bird is mainly seen on passage in Britain, where it frequents estuaries, saltings, marshes and lakes, and reservoirs with muddy margins. It breeds on bogs, often in open mature forest, in northern Europe, including the north of Scotland. Most of the population winters in Africa, but some birds do so in Britain and Ireland. The plumage is basically grey above, including the head and neck, and white below, becoming darker and more streaked in spring and summer. The long legs are greenish and the bill is quite stout and noticeably upcurved.

 Small invertebrates and also hunts fish in shallow water.

 Shallow, lined scrape on ground.

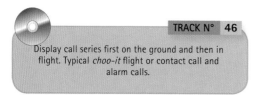

TRACK N° 46

Display call series first on the ground and then in flight. Typical *choo-it* flight or contact call and alarm calls.

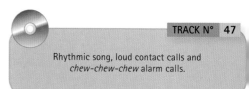

TRACK N° 47

Rhythmic song, loud contact calls and *chew-chew-chew* alarm calls.

48 | Curlew
Numenius arquata

This large grey-brown wader appears uniformly grey-brown at distance, but closer inspection reveals intricate patterns of light and dark streaking, along with dark arrow-head markings on the flanks of the adult. The outstanding feature, making identification straightforward, is the extremely long and down-curved bill, which is longer in the female and lacks the more sharply decurved tip of the closely related Whimbrel.

The species is a familiar sight in coastal areas in winter. In summer it breeds on moors, upland pastures and, more rarely nowadays, lowland wet meadows. It is known throughout the year for its loud and melancholy fluty *cur-lee* whistle, and in summer for a bubbling trill during its nuptial song flights.

It breeds across much of northern and central Europe, and in winter migrates as far south as the North African coast. It is resident and common in Britain.

 Molluscs and mud worms in winter, and insects and moorland berries in summer.

 Nests in a scrape on ground in grass tussocks or heather.

TRACK N° 48

Series of the frequently given *cur-lee* calls, and at the end the rising bubbling song that can be heard on the breeding grounds.

49 | Black-tailed Godwit
Limosa limosa

This large, long-legged wader with a long, straight bill breeds patchily throughout northern and central Europe on wet meadows and partially drained marshes. It is an uncommon breeding bird in Britain but occurs in large numbers on passage and in winter. It winters coastally in Britain and Atlantic coasts of Western Europe and Mediterranean, on estuaries, saltings, marshes and sheltered shores.

In spring the head, neck and breast become bright rufous-orange and the plumage as a whole brightens and darkens with rufous tints. In winter the plumage is a rather nondescript brownish-grey all over, except for a white belly and undertail.

However, the species is unmistakable at all times in flight, thanks to its startling black-and-white wing pattern, white rump and black tail. The closely related Bar-tailed Godwit has fairly plain dark-brownish wings and lacks the black on the tail; it is also shorter-legged and has a more upturned bill.

 Invertebrates, which it finds by probing the mud or sifting water with its long bill. Will take some plant matter, especially in winter.

Shallow scrape on ground in short vegetation.

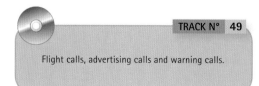

TRACK N° 49

Flight calls, advertising calls and warning calls.

50 | Temminck's Stint
Calidris temminckii

A very small, nondescript wader, it is brown-grey above and white below, with a grey, streaked breast and yellow legs; in summer it develops a variable scattering of black-centred and rufous-edged feathers on the back. Temminck's Stint is remarkable for delivering a trilling song during a hovering display flight. It is a summer visitor from Africa, with a breeding range mainly in northern Norway and Russia, where it is common on the tundra and mountains, although a few pairs breed sporadically in northern Scotland. Otherwise, it is a widespread but scarce visitor to Britain during migration.

 Mainly insects.

 Nest is a lined scrape in short grass.

51 | Dunlin
Calidris alpina

The Dunlin is common in winter and on migration along shores and estuaries. In summer most birds leave Britain, but a few remain to breed on high moors. Starling-sized, the Dunlin is grey above and white below, with the breast streaked darker, but in summer the upperparts become rufous-brown and a prominent black patch develops on the belly. At all times the rather long and gently decurved bill is a good identification feature.

 Small molluscs, crustaceans and worms in winter, but mainly insects in summer.

 A neat cup of grass, usually well hidden in a tussock.

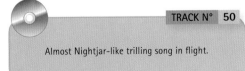

TRACK N° 50

Almost Nightjar-like trilling song in flight.

TRACK N° 51

Display calls: first a series of scolding, growling *churr'eeeer* ..., followed by a long, descending growling trill.

52 | Jack Snipe
Lymnocryptes minimus

53 | Great Snipe
Gallinago media

Smaller and shorter-billed than the Common Snipe, the Jack Snipe breeds on wet bogs in north-east Europe and winters on marshes with thick ground cover in from Britain and south to the Mediterranean. Like other snipe, the plumage is a mixture of browns and buffs, but the Jack Snipe can be identified by its small size, short bill, bold yellow stripes along the back and a greenish sheen to the mantle. It is very difficult to flush, but when disturbed it rises silently, usually only flying a short distance before alighting again in thick ground cover.

The Great Snipe is only a little larger than the Common Snipe, but much plumper bodied and with a shorter, thicker, bill. The plumage is very similar, but the barring on the belly is more extensive and it has obvious horizontal white barring on the closed wing. Its bulk and more rounded wings give it a heavier appearance in flight, and this is emphasized as it rises slowly and usually silently, often from almost underfoot. It breeds on wet meadows and marshy mountainsides in northern and north-eastern Europe. It migrates south-eastwards, so it is a rare bird in Western Europe and a vagrant to Britain.

 Insects, larvae, worms and seeds.

 Insects, larvae, earthworms and molluscs.

Nest is a lined cup on ground in short vegetation.

 Nest is a completely concealed shallow depression in thick vegetation.

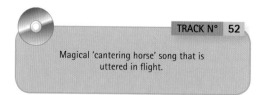

TRACK N° **52**

Magical 'cantering horse' song that is uttered in flight.

TRACK N° **53**

Nocturnal crackling calls at communal display lek.

54 | Common Snipe
Gallinago gallinago

This medium-sized wader has a disproportionately long bill. Its cryptic plumage is a mixture of browns and buffs, with a white belly and some dark barring on the flanks. It is prominently striped buff and black on the head. It is most easily distinguished from other species of snipe when flushed because it emits an explosive call and flies in a series of zig-zags before towering high into the sky.

The Common Snipe breeds across much of northern and central Europe, including Britain, in all manner of damp habitats, with northern and eastern breeders moving south and west for the winter.

When breeding, it performs a remarkable 'drumming' display flight where it plunges through the sky and forces air between its tail feathers – this results in a loud noise that is reminiscent of the bleating of a goat!

 Mainly worms and insects, which it locates by probing in mud with its long bill.

 Nest is a grass-lined cup in a tussock situated in boggy ground.

55 | Red-necked Phalarope
Phalaropus lobatus

This summer visitor to the far north of Europe includes a few pairs in the far north of Scotland. Elsewhere in Britain it is a scarce migrant on its way to and from its pelagic wintering grounds in the Indian Ocean. In summer, it is a dark slaty grey on the head, breast, flanks and back, with a white throat and red patch on the neck and upper breast. During breeding, the male's plumage is more subdued than the female's, and as phalaropes reverse roles, it is the male that incubates the eggs and raises the chicks. In winter the plumage is pale grey with a white neck and head, and an obvious solid black patch over and behind the eye. It feeds by spinning on the water.

 Small insects, plankton, larvae.

Nest in a tussock close to water.

56 | Black-headed Gull
Chroicocephalus ridibundus

This is a common and widespread small gull that is grey above and white below. Its name is a misnomer, because the head is actually chocolate-brown, and then only in the breeding season, with the dark colour decreasing to a mere ear-spot in winter. It may be abundant anywhere near water, including ponds in urban areas, where it will often readily come to take bread.

 Mainly invertebrates, but also grain and scraps.

Nests colonially, sometimes in large numbers, in tussocks or on flat ground by lakes, ponds and coastal marshes.

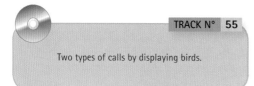

TRACK N° 55

Two types of calls by displaying birds.

TRACK N° 56

Slurred screeching calls, initially by a single individual, then the cacophony of a breeding colony. Very vocal, particularly at breeding colonies and feeding sites.

57 | Little Gull
Hydrocoloeus minutus

Our smallest gull is a winter visitor and passage migrant to Britain. It breeds colonially on freshwater marshes in north-eastern Europe, but winters at sea off the Atlantic and Mediterranean coasts of Europe. The adult is white with a grey mantle and white-tipped wings. In summer the head and neck are entirely black, with a dark red bill and bright scarlet legs. In winter the head becomes white with a grey crown and a black mark on the cheek. Rounded tips to the wings, which are almost black on the undersides, are very obvious in flight.

 Picks invertebrates from the surface of water. Also hawks for insects like a marsh tern.

Nests in vegetation by water.

58 | Common Gull
Larus canus

This medium-sized gull has a typical adult plumage of grey above, white below and black wing tips that have white spots called 'mirrors' on them. The legs and bill are greenish-yellow. Adult plumage is not attained until after the bird's second winter. Until then birds are, to varying degrees, browner on the wings and more streaked below. A resident in Britain, it breeds across northern Europe on marshes and shingle banks and by freshwater lakes and moorland lochs. Northern populations disperse south to winter on coasts, lakes and reservoirs.

 Molluscs, worms, insects and fish.

 Nest usually a lined scrape on the ground, but sometimes uses an elevated site, even in a tree.

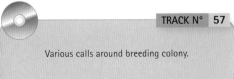

TRACK N° 57

Various calls around breeding colony.

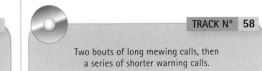

TRACK N° 58

Two bouts of long mewing calls, then a series of shorter warning calls.

59 | Black Tern
Chlidonias niger

This and the next two species are known as marsh terns (rather than sea terns). The Black Tern is a summer visitor to lowland lakes and marshes in Europe. It migrates through Britain, sometimes in good numbers, but only rarely breeds, and it winters on the coasts of tropical Africa. The body is black in summer, with a grey mantle, wings and tail. Its body becomes white in late summer, but retains a black cap that extends behind the eye, and in flight shows a distinctive blackish patch on the breast sides at the joint with the wing.

 Hawks over water like a giant Swallow, picking insects from the surface.

 Heap of rank vegetation often in very shallow water.

60 | White-winged Black Tern
Chlidonias leucopterus

This summer visitor from Africa frequents similar habitats to the Black Tern, but with a more easterly distribution in Europe. It is a rare visitor to Britain. Its plumage is like the Black Tern in summer, but the wings and tail are white, not grey, giving greater contrast. The two birds are very alike in winter plumage. However, the White-winged Black has less black on the head and is generally paler above than the Black, and it lacks the black marks on the sides of the breast.

 Mainly aquatic and flying invertebrates, often picked from the water's surface.

A mound of vegetation in shallow water.

TRACK N° 59

Chattering calls at breeding colony.

TRACK N° 60

Nasal *chuurk* calls at a colony.

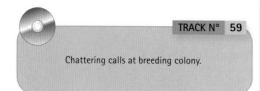

61 | Whiskered Tern
Chlidonias hybrida

Like the two previous species, this marsh tern winters in Africa, but it has a more southerly breeding distribution in Europe and is a vagrant to Britain. It is slightly larger and more robust than the other two species, with longer legs and a heavier bill. In breeding the plumage is a uniform pale-grey above and dark-grey below, with contrasting white cheeks, a black cap and bright red bill and legs. In winter it has a breast patch like the Black Tern, but this is less bold, and the Whiskered is generally paler on the upperparts.

 Insects, with occasional amphibians and small fish.

 Platform of aquatic vegetation anchored to a plant in, or very near, water.

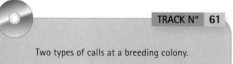

TRACK N° 61

Two types of calls at a breeding colony.

62 | Common Tern
Sterna hirundo

By far the commonest and most widespread member of its family in Europe, although it is classified as a sea tern, the Common Tern breeds on low-lying coasts and inland lakes and rivers across the continent. It is a common summer visitor to Britain and winters in Africa. It has a slender build, long, pointed wings and a long, deeply forked tail. The back and wings are grey and the underparts whitish. It has red legs, a red bill with a black tip, and a black cap with a forecrown that becomes white in winter.

 Plunge dives for small fish.

 A scrape on the ground; will readily nest on artificial floating rafts.

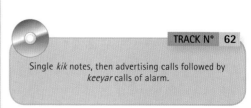

TRACK N° 62

Single *kik* notes, then advertising calls followed by *keeyar* calls of alarm.

63 | Kingfisher
Alcedo atthis

This colourful and charismatic bird is a common resident throughout much of Europe except for the far north, although birds that breed in Eastern Europe move south in the winter. It breeds around lowland, fish-rich streams, slow-flowing rivers and canals, and lakes, preferably with overhanging branches on which to perch and fish from. On migration and in winter it is found in a wider variety of wetland habitats including estuaries, sheltered coasts and harbours.

The Kingfisher is about the same size as a Starling, and it is dumpy, with a large bill. The plumage is iridescent, pale turquoise-blue on the back, with greenish-blue wings and orange underparts. The birds often sit motionless for long periods on a favoured perch, but are more usually seen as a flash of brilliant colour speeding over the water. Its high-pitched piping call is often the first clue as to its presence.

 Mainly small fish, especially sticklebacks, caught by diving from a low perch.

 Excavates a tunnel, up to a metre long, in a sand or earth bank.

TRACK N° 63

Song comprising high-pitched notes, calls in flight and perched, plus 'splash' sound by diving bird.

64 | Sand Martin
Riparia riparia

A summer visitor from Africa, this is the only brown-backed martin found in Britain. It is white below and has a distinctive brownish breast band separating the white throat and breast. A colonial breeder around sand and gravel pits, and also where other suitable banks exist (rivers and cliffs), it feeds aerially by catching tiny insects, usually over water. On migration it roosts communally in reed beds.

 Small insects, which are taken on the wing.

Excavates a tunnel up to a metre long in sand or earth bank.

65 | Swallow
Hirundo rustica

This bird is a common sight in the countryside around rivers, lakes, farms and villages, and is notable for its long tail streamers. It has blue-black upperparts and pale buff underparts, which are relieved only by a bright chestnut chin. Summer visitors to Britain from southern Africa, Swallows frequently line telegraph wires in autumn before flying south.

Almost exclusively insects taken on the wing. Often hunts low over water.

Originally a cup of mud in a cave or on rocks, but has evolved to nest close to man on outbuildings, porches and sheds instead.

 TRACK N° 64

Churring calls at breeding colony, then more subdued calls by a large flock of feeding birds.

 TRACK N° 65

Melodious twittering song, interspersed with a strangled croak, followed by a trilling rattle. Then subsong of flock of perched migrants, followed by calls of fledged juveniles.

66 | Bearded Tit
Panurus biarmicus

Although it closely resembles species from the tit family, the latest genetic research suggests that the Bearded Tit is most closely related to the larks. It is generally a resident reed-bed specialist and this limits the species' distribution in Europe. In Britain it occurs mostly in southern England and East Anglia. However, in autumn it does undertake sporadic short-distance migrations known as 'eruptions' in search of new reed beds. The plumage is tawny-brown overall, with black and white patches in the wings, a yellow eye and a long tail. Males have a blue-grey head with a black 'beard' patch running from the eye down to the neck.

 Reed seeds plus insects and spiders in summer.

 Nest built of reed stems and situated low in reeds over shallow water.

67 | Penduline Tit
Remiz pendulinus

This tiny bird frequents wetland areas of central and Eastern Europe and coastal marshes of the Mediterranean. It requires proximal trees in which to nest. It is seen with increasing regularity in England and is resident in southern Europe, but northern breeding populations migrate south in autumn. It has rich brown back and is buff-grey below, with red-brown spotting on the male's breast. Both sexes have grey heads with a black eye mask that is bolder on the male and absent altogether on the juvenile. Very small and unobtrusive, its presence is often first detected through hearing the distinctive call.

 Food mainly insects.

Nest a pouch-shaped structure suspended from the end of a tree branch, often over water.

TRACK N° 66

Various typical pinging, chipping and buzzing calls.

TRACK N° 67

Drawn-out *seeeuu* calls, followed by the simple trilling, warbling song.

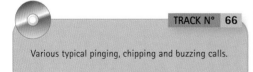

68 | Cetti's Warbler
Cettia cetti

It has a rather uniform plumage of warm dark brown above and dark grey below, with a broad rounded, often cocked, tail. It is very unobtrusive and difficult to even glimpse, so the best clue to its presence is often the loud, explosive song. Mainly resident in areas of dense vegetation, it is usually, but by no means always, near water. Formerly confined to southern Europe, it extended its range north into much of France, and more recently Britain, in the last century.

 Chiefly insects.

 Builds a bulky, untidy cup in thick vegetation.

69 | Moustached Warbler
Acrocephalus melanopogon

The Moustached Warbler is superficially similar in appearance to the Sedge Warbler, but overall more brownish-red with rusty-brown flanks and sides to the breast, a blackish cap and a well-defined white throat. It is confined to southern Europe, where it is resident in the west, but it is a short-distance migrant in the east of its range. It has never occurred in Britain. It is found in areas of reed and bulrush, where it is very unobtrusive and difficult to see as it moves low in the vegetation or on the ground.

 Mainly invertebrates, including many arthropods and snails.

Well-concealed cup in tall aquatic vegetation over swampy ground.

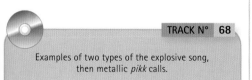

TRACK N° 68

Examples of two types of the explosive song, then metallic *pikk* calls.

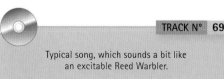

TRACK N° 69

Typical song, which sounds a bit like an excitable Reed Warbler.

70 | Sedge Warbler
Acrocephalus schoenabaenus

This small bird is brown above with darker streaking, and has a plain rufous rump, unmarked buff-white underparts and a bold black-bordered creamy stripe above the eye. When seen singing at close range, it has a conspicuous red gape. It either sings from a perch or employs an oft-repeated song flight, rising vertically from vegetation with a series of excitable, harsh chattering phrases, before quickly dropping back into cover again.

A summer visitor to Britain from sub-Saharan Africa, the Sedge Warbler is common where there is thick vegetation close to water, and has a preference for small ponds, ditches and marshy areas.

It breeds in most parts of northern and central Europe in a variety of wetland habitats ranging from damp meadows and reed beds to riverbanks and well-vegetated margins of lakes and gravel pits.

Gnats, midges, aquatic insects and small molluscs. Also eats berries in autumn, when it is building up fat reserves in preparation for migration.

A neat shallow cup of grass and moss is constructed about a metre off ground in tangled low herbage, usually near water.

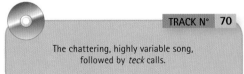

TRACK N° 70

The chattering, highly variable song, followed by *teck* calls.

71 | Reed Warbler
Acrocephalus scirpaceus

As its name suggests, the Reed Warbler is largely confined to reed beds during the breeding season, although it can occur in other habitats such as nettle-beds and crops, but on migration can be found much more widely in a variety of damp, well-vegetated situations.

The plumage is rather nondescript brown above and buff below. It has a relatively long bill and a distinctive flat crown, which combined with the rather long, rounded tail often give it an elongated appearance. It is most often seen singing as it climbs up a reed stem.

A summer visitor from tropical Africa to reed-bed habitat in across Europe, except in the far north, in Britain it breeds widely in England and Wales, but is a scarce migrant in Scotland.

 Small aquatic insects. In autumn it feeds on berries, which provide energy for its long migratory flight.

Intricately woven grass structure affixed around three reed stems growing out of water.

TRACK N° 71

Song consisting of phrases repeated in groups of three or more – *kek kek kek, ker ker ker, tri tri tri*. Then typical *cherk* calls.

72 | Marsh Warbler
Acrocephalus palustris

Almost identical to the Reed Warbler, the Marsh Warbler is best distinguished by song and habitat. It is a summer visitor from tropical Africa to mainly central and eastern parts of Europe. It avoids reed beds, preferring rank vegetation with nettles, cow parsley and meadowsweet on the edges of ditches, canals, slow-moving rivers and marshes. It has unobtrusive habits except when singing, and the fine differences in plumage between it and the Reed Warbler are difficult to observe in the field. It is very scarce in Britain, even on passage.

 Mainly insects with some seeds.

 Cylindrical cup of leaves and grass in tall, dense vegetation.

73 | Great Reed Warbler
Acrocephalus arundinaceus

This very large warbler, almost the size of a Song Thrush, is very similar in plumage to the Reed Warbler, but with a more prominent supercilium and a much heavier-looking bill. It is a summer visitor from tropical Africa found mainly in reed beds, but also in other tall, dense vegetation, throughout Europe, being absent only from Britain, the far north and upland areas. It is a rare vagrant to Britain. Best located by its very loud, far-carrying song.

 Mainly invertebrates.

Cup of reed stems woven around thick reeds.

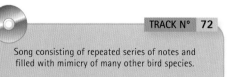

TRACK N° 72

Song consisting of repeated series of notes and filled with mimicry of many other bird species.

TRACK N° 73

Typical deep song consisting of repeated notes: *choo-choo-choo, ker-ker-ker, kirrick- kirrick- kirrick...*

74 | Savi's Warbler
Locustella luscinioides

In its usual habitat of extensive reed beds, the Savi's Warbler is often best located thanks to its deep, reeling song. It is a summer visitor with a patchy distribution throughout Europe, but it is a very rare breeder in Britain and absent from Fenno-Scandinavia. The plumage is warm brown above and buff-white below, and it has a broad, rounded tail with pale-tipped, reddish-buff markings on the underside. It spends much of its time on the ground creeping among reed stems and is difficult to see except when singing from an often exposed reed stem.

 Invertebrates including insects and small snails.

 Well-concealed cup in aquatic vegetation.

75 | Bluethroat
Luscinia svecica

Brown above and whitish below, the male Bluethroat has a bold white eye-stripe and a blue throat with a red or white central spot, and bands of black, white and chestnut on the lower border. These colours are more restricted and subdued in females and immatures. A summer visitor from Africa and Asia, birds with red throat patches breed in Scandinavia, while those with white patches breed in other parts of Europe. In Britain the species is a scarce passage migrant. It is found in a variety of habitats, but always close to water. It is skulking on passage, when it is most frequently seen hopping on marshy ground or in a ditch, with a characteristically cocked tail.

 Insects with some seeds and berries.

 Cup of grass in a tussock.

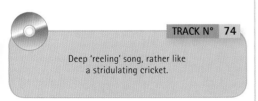

TRACK N° 74

Deep 'reeling' song, rather like a stridulating cricket.

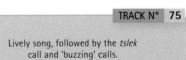

TRACK N° 75

Lively song, followed by the *tslek* call and 'buzzing' calls.

76 | Yellow Wagtail
Motacilla flava

Slim and long-tailed like all wagtails, this summer visitor from Africa has a green-brown back and yellow underparts, which are bright in the male and less so in the female. Immatures are more or less brown above and whitish with a hint of yellow below.

The colour of the head of the breeding male is dictated by geography. In Britain the Yellow Wagtail's head is greenish-brown with a yellow supercilium and throat. The head of the continental European subspecies, the Blue-headed Wagtail, is blue-grey with a white supercilium and sub-moustachial stripe. The Grey-headed Wagtail, the subspecies occurring in Fenno-Scandinavia, has a dark grey crown and nape with blackish ear-coverts.

The species frequents lowland areas, especially damp meadows, pastures with cattle and marshland edges. Hearing the distinctive *tseep* call is often the first indication of its presence. In Britain it is a much declined but still fairly common bird in England and Wales but absent from much of Scotland.

 Mainly insects, larvae and small snails.

 Constructs a nest of grass and moss lined with hair in a grass tussock.

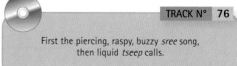

TRACK N° 76

First the piercing, raspy, buzzy *sree* song, then liquid *tseep* calls.

77 | Citrine Wagtail
Motacilla citreola

This summer visitor from South-East Asia breeds in wet meadows and bogs in the far east of Europe, but in recent years its range has gradually extended west into Poland and the Baltic States. It is a vagrant to Britain. The male has a bright lemon-yellow head and underparts, with a black shawl around the nape, grey upperparts and blackish wings that show two prominent white wing-bars. The female is similar but with a grey crown, dark mask through the eye and yellow restricted to the breast and flanks.

 Mainly aquatic invertebrates.

 A lined cup situated in vegetation on the ground.

78 | Grey Wagtail
Motacilla cinerea

The Grey Wagtail is a striking bird with a very long tail that is constantly in motion. It is grey above and white below, with bright yellow on the breast, rump and undertail. It is fairly common in Western Europe, including Britain, where there are fast-flowing rivers and streams with exposed rocks on which to perch. Although mainly resident, in winter it often moves to lower ground around lakes, slow-flowing rivers and estuaries.

 Mainly insects and small crustaceans.

 Builds a nest of grass and other vegetation in a rock crevice, bank, bridge or building, always situated close to running water.

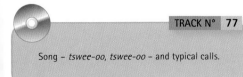

TRACK N° 77

Song – *tswee-oo, tswee-oo* – and typical calls.

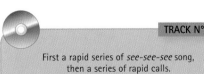

TRACK N° 78

First a rapid series of *see-see-see* song, then a series of rapid calls.

79 | Pied Wagtail
Motacilla alba

This black-and-white wagtail (subspecies *Motacilla alba yarrelli*), with a long, often wagged tail, is a familiar sight throughout Britain, even in the hearts of cities. It is resident and found only in Britain and the near Continent. In the rest of Europe it is replaced by its close relative, the White Wagtail (subspecies *M. a. alba*), which has a pale grey rather than black back. This subspecies also occurs in Britain on passage in small numbers, particularly in spring.

On the ground, the Pied Wagtail's gait is rapid, and it moves its head backwards and forwards while wagging its tail. It runs rapidly on the ground after flying insects, preferring to feed on lawns and roofs, and in car parks and roads, where its prey is easily spotted.

Outside the breeding season, the Pied Wagtail roosts gregariously – dozens or even hundreds of birds can often be seen going to roost in trees and on buildings in towns and cities.

 Insects.

Constructs a nest of grass and roots, lined with animal hair, usually in a recess in a wall or building. Both sexes build the nest and incubate the eggs.

TRACK N° 79

First the slowly advancing (with long pauses) song of *tsitsellittt* notes, then some disyllabic *tsli-vitt* calls, often given when taking flight.

80 | Reed Bunting
Emberiza schoeniclus

The breeding male Reed Bunting is unmistakable, with a black head and throat, and a white moustache and neck collar, but in winter only vestiges of this distinctive plumage remain and it becomes a basically brown-above, white-below bird, streaked darker all over, like the female. All plumages display a bold moustachial stripe and white outer-tail feathers.

Reed Buntings are resident in Britain and widely distributed wherever there are reed stands, marshes and bushy areas with damp ground. In winter they are often found – along with other buntings and sparrows – around farmland, where food is easier to find. It is mainly resident in Western Europe, with short-distance migration south and west of birds that breed in more northerly and central parts.

 Mainly insects in summer, and seeds and grain in winter.

Forms a nest of grass, reed blades and moss close to the ground in a tussock or low bush.

TRACK N° 80
Rapid song by unpaired male, then a slower halting, barely musical version with pauses between notes. Calls include a downwards-inflected *tseeou* and a nasal rasping *djuh*.

Other Natural History Books by New Holland Publishers

Advanced Bird ID Handbook:
The Western Palearctic
Nils van Duivendijk. Award-winning and innovative field guide covering the key features of every important plumage of all 1,350 species and subspecies that have ever occurred in Britain, Europe, North Africa and the Middle East. Published in association with the journal *British Birds*. £24.99 ISBN 978 1 78009 022 1.
Also available: **Advanced Bird ID Guide: The Western Palearctic** £14.99 ISBN 978 1 84773 607 9.

Bill Oddie's Birds of Britain & Ireland
Bill Oddie. A new and fully updated edition of this popular title. Ideal for any birder coming to grips with the 200 or so most common species. Written in Bill's own inimitable style, the book includes all the latest updates, while a unique feature is the 10 pages featuring 'confusion species'. £12.99 ISBN 978 1 78009 245 4

Birds: Magic Moments
Markus Varesvuo. Bringing together the work of one of the world's best bird photographers, this is a celebration of the avian world, illustrating rarely observed scenes from courtship, nest-building, hunting and raising young. The author's stunning images cover species ranging from colourful bee-eaters to majestic eagles. £20 ISBN 978 1 78009 075 7
Also available: **Fascinating Birds** £20, ISBN 978 1 78009 178 5.

New Holland Concise Bird Guide
An ideal first field guide to British birds for children or adults. Includes more than 250 species and 800 colour artworks. Published in association with The Wildlife Trusts. £4.99 ISBN 978 1 84773 601 7.
Other Concise Guides include (all £4.99): **Butterfly and Moth** ISBN 978 1 84773 602 4, **Garden Bird** ISBN 978 1 84773 978 0, **Garden Wildlife** ISBN 978 1 84773 606 2, **Herb** ISBN 978 1 84773 976 6, **Insect** ISBN 978 1 84773 604 8, **Mushroom** ISBN 978 1 84773 785 4, **Pond Wildlife** ISBN 978 1 84773 977 3, **Seashore Wildlife** ISBN 978 1 84773 786 1, **Tree** ISBN 978 1 84773 605 5 and **Wild Flower** ISBN 978 1 84773 603 1.

New Holland European Bird Guide
Peter H Barthel. The only truly pocket-sized comprehensive field guide to all the birds of Britain and Europe. Features more than 1,700 beautiful and accurate artworks of more than 500 species. £10.99 ISBN 978 1 84773 110 4.

Peregrine Falcon
Patrick Stirling-Aird. Beautifully illustrated book detailing the life of this remarkable raptor, and offering a window into a rarely seen world. Contains more than 80 stunning colour photographs. £14.99 ISBN 978 1 84773 769 4.
Also available: **Barn Owl** (£14.99, ISBN 978 1 84773 768 7). **Kingfisher** (£12.99, ISBN 978 1 84773 524 9).

See www.newhollandpublishers.com for more than 200 Natural History titles

Track Listing

Index

Roman type = English name
Italic type = Latin name